More "Why" Stories

A Dolch Classic Basic Reading Book

by Edward W. Dolch and Marguerite P. Dolch

illustrated by Alex Bloch

The Basic Reading Books

The Basic Reading Books are fun reading books that fill the need for easy-to-read stories for the primary grades. The interest appeal of these folktales and legends will encourage independent reading at the early reading levels.

The stories focus on the 95 Common Nouns and the Dolch 220 Basic Sight Vocabulary. Beyond these simple lists, the books use about two or three new words per page.

This series was prepared under the direction and supervision of Edward W. Dolch, Ph.D.

This revision was prepared under the direction and supervision of Eleanor Dolch LaRoy and the Dolch Family Trust.

SRA/McGraw-Hill

*A Division of The **McGraw·Hill** Companies*

Send all inquiries to:
SRA/McGraw-Hill
250 Old Wilson Bridge Road, Suite 310
Worthington, OH 43085

ISBN 0-02-830817-4

2 3 4 5 6 7 8 9 0 QST 04 03 02 01 00 99

Table of Contents

Why the Woodpecker Looks for Bugs 5

Why the Stork Has No Tail 9

The Gentle People 19

Why the Water Buffalo Has a Split Hoof 25

Why the Squirrel Lives in Trees 31

How Three Tails Came to Be As They Are

    Now, Part I 37

How Three Tails Came to Be As They Are

    Now, Part II 45

Why the Woodpecker Looks for Bugs

Once upon a time the woodpecker was an old woman with a long nose. She was not a very kind old woman. She was not good to the children who lived on her street. And she always wanted to know about everything that was going on.

One day an old man walked down the street. He had a big, big bag. He came upon the old woman.

"Old Woman," he said, "will you please take this bag to your house? But do not open it. I will come back for it."

"I will do what you say," said the old woman. "I will take the big bag to my house, and I will not open it."

But as soon as the man had gone,
the old woman opened the bag.

Bugs and more bugs came out of the
bag. Bugs ran all around. Bugs and more
bugs ran over the grass. Bugs and more
bugs ran up the trees.

The old woman wished she had not opened the bag. She did not know what to do. She started to pick up the bugs and put them back into the bag. All day long she picked up bugs and more bugs and put them back into the bag. But there were bugs everywhere. She could not pick them all up.

When the sun had gone down, the old woman was very tired. She went back to her house. And there sat the old man by her door.

"Old Woman, where is the big bag that I gave you to keep for me?" said the old man.

"Here it is," said the old woman. And oh, how she wished that she had not opened that bag and let the bugs out.

"You have opened this bag," said the old man. "Where are all the bugs that I had in this big bag?"

"The bugs are in the grass. The bugs are in the trees. All day long I have been picking up bugs and putting them into the bag," said the old woman. "But I cannot get all the bugs back into the bag."

Then, the old man, who was magic, said, "Old Woman, you shall be a woodpecker. All day long you shall pick up bugs. And never again can you be a woman."

And that is why the woodpecker picks up bugs all day long. The woodpecker is trying to find all the bugs that got out of that big bag.

Why the Stork Has No Tail

One day the king of the storks called all the storks to come to him. And he told them this story:

"When I was young," said the king of the storks, "I was put into a big cage. A kind man came by and saw me in the cage. 'No man should kill a stork,' he said. And he opened the cage and let me out. I said to this kind man, 'My life is your life. When you call, I will come to you. And I will give my life for your life.'

"Today the man called me, and I went to him. He has asked me to get for him the Water of Life. And I do not know where to find the Water of Life. If I cannot find the Water of Life for this man, I shall have to give my life for his life.

"Is there any one of the storks who knows where to find the Water of Life?" asked the king.

Then, an old, old stork who had only one eye and a hurt leg came up to the king of the storks.

"My good king," said the old stork, "When I was young, I flew to where the mountains knock together. And it is where the mountains knock together that you will find the Water of Life. It was there that my eye was put out, and I hurt my leg. I can show the young storks the mountains that knock together.

"Who will go with this old stork and bring back to me the Water of Life?" asked the king.

All the storks looked at the old, old stork with only one eye and with a hurt leg. No one of the storks wanted to go to the mountains that knock together and get the Water of Life.

The king of the storks asked again, "Who will go with this old stork and bring back to me the Water of Life?"

But all of the young storks turned away.

"I am very old, but I would be happy to give my life for the king," said the old stork with only one eye and a hurt leg. "Let me go again to the mountains that knock together and get for you the Water of Life."

"Old stork," said the king, "can you fly that far?"

"I can try," said the old stork. "Tie a bottle to my leg so that I can bring back the Water of Life."

The king tied a bottle to the leg of the old stork. And the old stork flew far, far away. The old stork flew to where the mountains were. But he was so tired that he had to sit down. And as he was sitting on a stone, a little bird came up to him.

"Go away," said the little bird. "The mountains will kill you."

"I cannot go away," said the old stork. "I have come to get the Water of Life that is by the mountains that knock together."

And then, the old stork told the little bird the story about the king of the storks.

"I must help you," said the little bird. "Do not forget what I say to you. When the sun is over the tops of the mountains, the mountains go to sleep. They do not sleep very long. But at that time you can fill your bottle with the Water of Life. You must fly up right away. And do not touch the mountains. Do not touch so much as one little stone."

"I shall do as you say," said the old stork, "and my king will thank you for the help that you have given me."

The little bird flew away, and the old stork watched the tops of the mountains that knock together.

When the sun was over the tops of the mountains, the old stork flew to the mountains. He filled the bottle with the Water of Life. Then, the old stork flew up again. But as he flew up, he touched a little stone on one of the mountains.

The mountains knocked together to hold the old stork by the tail. The old stork pulled, and he pulled. And he pulled his tail right out.

"What is a tail?" said the old stork to himself, as he flew back to the king. "I have my life and I have a bottle of the Water of Life for my king."

When the old stork came to the king of the storks, the other storks laughed at him. They laughed, and they laughed at the old stork with only one eye and a hurt leg and no tail.

The king of the storks said to the other storks, "Why do you laugh at this old stork? He is better than you. He was willing to give his life for me. And now he brings me a bottle of the Water of Life, that I may give it to the man who let me out of the cage when I was young."

But the old stork looked so funny without a tail, that the other storks just laughed and laughed.

"Look at your own tails," cried the king of the storks. "Look at your own tails."

And every stork looked where his own tail had been. But not one stork had a tail.

And from that time to this, no stork has had a tail.

The Gentle People

In a far, far away time, in the mountains of South America, there lived a Gentle People who loved the flowers and the birds and the animals.

Their children were as beautiful as the flowers and the birds. The children were kind to all living things. The Gentle People would never fight. They never killed anything that lived.

The king of the Gentle People could do great magic. He could turn people into flowers or birds or animals. Sometimes he would turn himself into a bird just so that he could fly over the trees.

Sometimes the children would ask the king to turn them into beautiful flowers so that the sun could warm them. Sometimes when the children would want to run on the mountains, they would ask the king to turn them into *guanacos*. A *guanaco* is a gentle animal like a sheep that lives in the mountains in South America.

The Gentle People lived together, and they did not fight, and they did not kill. They loved everything that was alive. They had beautiful clothes. And they loved everything.

There was only one thing that the Gentle People could not do. They could not go into the woods. No one went into the woods.

But one day, one of the Gentle People, called Capa, saw a beautiful bird. Capa had never seen a bird like this one. He had never seen a bird that he could not hold in his hand. This bird flew away. Capa went after the bird, because he wanted to get it for the king. The bird flew into the far woods. Capa went after it.

For a day and night Capa went after the beautiful bird. But he could not put his hands on it.

After a long time, Capa came out of the woods. He saw many creatures who looked to him like big monkeys. These creatures took away Capa's beautiful clothes. Then, they began to fight to see who would keep the beautiful clothes they had taken from Capa.

Capa turned and ran. He never stopped running, day or night. And when he got to the king, he told him of the creatures like big monkeys who fight and kill.

The king called all the Gentle People to come before him. He talked to them and told them of the creatures like monkeys who fight and kill.

"They have seen our Capa," said the king. "Now they will come to fight and kill us and to take all our beautiful things."

"What are we to do?" cried the Gentle People.

"I could show you how to fight," said the king, "and then you could fight these creatures. But that will do you no good. Because after you have killed the monkey creatures, you will kill flowers and birds and animals. You will fight over beautiful clothes and other beautiful things."

"What are we to do? What are we to do?" cried the Gentle People. "We love the birds and the animals. They are our friends. We do not want to kill them."

"By my magic," said the king, "I can turn you into guanacos."

"Yes, yes," cried the Gentle People. "Turn us into guanacos, because a guanaco will not hurt any living thing. Then we can go and live far away in the mountains, and the monkey creatures will never find us."

So the king turned his people into guanacos, and he turned himself into the biggest guanaco of all so he could look after them. That is why, when the guanacos are eating, one big guanaco is always looking after the others.

When the monkey creatures came out of the woods to fight and kill, the Gentle People were not there. But the monkey creatures saw many, many guanacos running away to the mountains.

And some day, when there is no more fighting and killing, the guanacos may come down from the mountains and turn back into the Gentle People.

Why the Water Buffalo Has a Split Hoof

Once upon a time, when the animals talked together just as people do now, the turtle was walking in the woods. He saw the water buffalo.

The turtle, who was very small, looked at the water buffalo, who was very big, and he said to himself, "If I could just get this water buffalo to be my friend, I know that he could help me. He is so big, and I am so little."

"Good day to you, my friend," said the turtle to the water buffalo.

But the water buffalo did not say a thing to the turtle.

Then, the turtle said to the water buffalo, "I have been thinking that it is not a good thing to live all by myself. My good friend, will you come and live with me?"

The water buffalo stopped. He looked at the turtle in the grass.

"Live with you," said the water buffalo. "Why, I am a big water buffalo, and you are nothing but a little turtle."

"I cannot help being little," said the turtle. "But I can think faster than you can. And I can run faster, too. Will you run a race with me?"

"What! A water buffalo run a race with a turtle?" said the water buffalo, and he laughed and laughed.

"Well, if you will not run a race with me," said the turtle, "I shall tell all the animals in the woods that you are afraid. You are afraid to run a race with a turtle."

The water buffalo did not like this. He did not want all the other animals in the woods to think that he was afraid of anything. So he said to the turtle, "In three days, I will run a race with you. We shall race over the road of the seven hills. And my hoofs will go up and down so fast that you cannot see them. I can run over seven hills in the time it will take you to walk over one hill." And the water buffalo ran off into the woods.

The turtle went to see his turtle friends, and he told them about the race with the water buffalo.

"If you will help me," he said, "we can win this race. Then the animals in the woods will no longer laugh at the turtles, because they cannot run fast with their little legs."

The other turtles said that they would help. And then the turtle who was going to run the race took seven turtles with him who were just as big as he was. He took them to the road of the seven hills. On every hill, he put a turtle and he told them just what to do.

On the day of the race, the turtle and the water buffalo went to the road of the seven hills. All the animals in the woods were there to watch the race.

"This is the day of the race," said the water buffalo. "And it will be a funny thing to see a water buffalo race with a turtle."

"Yes," said the turtle. "It will be a funny race. Let us be off."

They started off down the road of the seven hills. The water buffalo ran very fast. When he looked back, he could not see the turtle. But when he got to the top of the first hill, there was a turtle ahead of him.

"Here I am," called the turtle. "You must run faster to win this race."

The water buffalo ran as fast as he could run. His hoofs went up and down so fast that you could not see them. But at the top of every hill, he saw a turtle ahead of him.

And when he got to the top of the seventh hill, there was a turtle. And the turtle called, "Here I am. You must run faster if you want to win this race."

When the water buffalo got to the end of the race, he saw a turtle there before him. He was so angry to think he had lost the race. He hit the turtle with his hoof. The turtle's shell kept the turtle from being hurt. But the old water buffalo split his hoof on the shell of the turtle. And to this very day, the water buffalo has a split hoof.

Why the Squirrel Lives in Trees

Once upon a time, the wolf and the dog were very good friends. The wolf lived in the woods. The dog lived on the farm. But every day the wolf and the dog played together.

But one day the wolf said to the dog, "Friend Dog, my teeth are longer than your teeth."

The dog said, "Friend Wolf, your teeth are longer than my teeth, but my teeth are stronger than your teeth."

At this the wolf gave an angry growl. "Dog, Dog, not so fast," said the wolf. "You know that in every way I am stronger than you are."

"Well," said the dog, and he gave an angry growl, "we will see about that. You get the animals that live in the woods to be on your side. I will get the animals that live on the farm to be on my side."

"Yes," said the wolf. "We will do just that. I know that the animals who live in the woods are stronger than the animals that live on the farm."

"Today, when the sun is over the treetops, we will see," said the dog.

The wolf ran into the woods. He called the bear and the fox and the rabbit and the squirrel.

"Come with me," cried the wolf. "We are going to see who is strongest—the animals that live in the woods or the animals that live on the farm."

The dog ran to the farm and called the cow and the pig and the hen and the cat.

"Come with me," cried the dog. "We are going to see who is strongest—the animals that live in the woods or the animals that live on the farm."

Then, the dog said to his friends, "I know that the bear is stronger than we are. But if we work together, we can scare the bear away. Cat, you jump on the bear's head and cover his eyes. Hen, you stand on his foot and peck his toes. Cow, you push him with your horns. Pig, you can pull his tail. I will nip at his heels."

And that is just what they did. The cat jumped on the bear's head and covered his eyes. The hen stood on his foot and pecked his toes. The cow pushed him with her horns. The pig pulled his tail. The dog nipped at his heels.

When the other animals came out of the woods, they saw that the cat was on the bear's head, covering his eyes. The hen was standing on his foot and pecking his toes. The cow was pushing him with her horns. The pig was pulling his tail, and the dog was nipping at his heels.

"Help, help," cried the bear. "Someone is trying to kill me."

The bear wanted to fight, but the animals did not let go.

"Help, help, help," cried the bear. And he ran away into the woods as fast as he could go.

Now, the bear is bigger than the wolf or the fox or the rabbit or the squirrel. And when the bear ran away, the other animals from the woods were afraid.

The wolf and the fox and the rabbit ran away into the woods. But the squirrel ran up into a tree.

The squirrel said to himself, "If the animals on the farm are stronger than the biggest animal in the woods, I had better get up here in the tree."

The squirrel was afraid to come down from the tree. And from that day to this, the squirrel lives up in a tree.

How Three Tails Came to Be as They are Now
Part I

Once upon a time, the rat had a beautiful tail like the tail of a horse. The deer had a tail like the tail of a dog. The rabbit's tail was long like the tail of a cat.

That was the time when a wizard lived in the woods. The old wizard used his magic to hurt people that he did not like.

On one side of the woods there lived a man who had two sons. The two boys were good and brave. They could work better than any two men. And they could sing better than the birds in the woods.

One day, the father said to his two sons, "My boys, you are big now, and it is time that you cut down trees in the woods and made a farm of your own."

"Where shall we go to cut down the trees and make a farm of our own?" asked the boys.

"I think," said the father, "that you could make a good farm on the other side of the woods."

As soon as the sun was up, the boys went to the other side of the woods. All day long they cut down big trees. They worked hard, and as they worked, they liked to sing.

The birds came to hear the boys sing. A lizard who was as big as a man came out of the woods so that he could hear the boys sing.

"These are good boys," said the big lizard to himself. "See how they work. And they sing as they work. I am glad that they have come to my side of the woods.

An old wizard who lived there was not glad.

"I must make these boys go away from my woods." said the old wizard to himself.

The old wizard thought of all the magic things that he could do. But he did not know of any way that he could make the boys go out of his woods. And so the old wizard went to see the owl.

The wizard told the owl that they must make the boys get out of their woods. And the owl sat in the tree and thought a long time.

Then, the owl said to the old wizard, "You must make the father think that the boys are not working, but only singing and playing. The father will get angry and not let them have the farm."

The old wizard put on his long, black coat. He flew up over the treetops to the other side of the woods. And when he got to the other side of the woods, he took off his long, black coat, and he went out of the woods. He walked up the father and said, "Good day to you, my man."

"Good day to you," said the father. "From where do you come?"

"I come from the other side of the woods," said the old wizard.

"Then you may have seen my sons who are cutting down trees to make a farm of their own," said the father.

"I saw two boys who were singing and playing," said the old wizard.

The father did not know what to think. He said to the old wizard, "What can I do with two boys who do not work?"

"If they were my boys," said the old wizard, "I would not let them have the farm."

With that, the old wizard walked away. And when the father could not see him, the old wizard put on his long, black coat. And then, he flew up over the trees to his side of the woods.

When the sun had gone down, the boys came back to their father. But they found that their father was very angry.

"Why did you sing and play all day?" said the father. "I told you to cut down trees and make a farm of your own."

And nothing that the boys could say would make their father think that they had not played, but had cut down trees all day long.

"When the sun is up," said the father, "you will go again to the woods and cut down ten times ten big trees."

As soon as the sun was up, the two boys went to the other side of the woods. And all day long, they worked as they had never worked before. They cut down ten times ten big trees. They had little time to sing. The birds and the big lizard up in the trees watched them. And when the sun had gone down, the boys were very tired when they got back to their father.

"Father," said the boys, "We have cut down ten times ten big trees today. And we are very tired. May we eat and then go to sleep?"

"Yes," said the father. "I am glad to know that you have worked today. When the sun comes up, I will go with you to the other side of the woods and see what you have done."

The owl, who was up in a tree, heard what the father said. He flew back to the old wizard, and he said, "Old wizard, now is the time to do some of your magic. When the sun is up, the father will come to see all the trees that the boys have cut down today."

The old wizard sat down, and he thought of all the magic things that he could do. Then, he said to the owl, "Go and get the rat and the deer and the rabbit. We have much work to do, and I want them to help me with my magic."

All night long the rat and the deer and rabbit worked with the old wizard. They put the trees back up in the woods again. And in the morning the woods looked just it had before the two boys had started to cut down the trees.

When the sun was up, the father and his two sons went to the other side of the woods. They could not find where one tree had been cut down in the woods. The boys did not know what to say. And the father was very, very angry.

How Three Tails Came to Be as They are Now
Part II

The father had told his two boys to cut down trees on the other side of the woods to make a farm. They had cut down many trees, but the old wizard had put the trees up again. So the father thought the boys had not been working. He was very angry.

"How can my sons tell me that they cut down trees all day? I can see with my own eyes that the trees are growing in the woods. Not a tree has been cut down."

"Father, Father," cried the boys. "We know that there must be some magic here. For we know that all day long we cut down trees. We worked all day, and we cut down ten times ten big trees."

"Very well," said the father. "Cut down ten times ten big trees today." The father went back to his house, and he was very, very angry.

When he got back to his house, there was the old wizard. He said to the father, "Good day to you, my man. Did I not tell you that your sons were singing and playing all day? If they were my boys, I would not let them have the farm."

"It may be so," said the father. "I will go to the other side of the woods before the sun goes down. And if my sons have not cut down ten times ten big trees, I will not let them have the farm. But if they have cut down ten times ten big trees, I will run you out of the woods."

The two boys started to cut down the big trees. But they were so tired that they could not work very well. It took them a long time to cut down just one tree.

Now the big lizard saw everything that went on in the woods. He had seen that the old wizard and the rat and the deer and rabbit had worked all night long putting the trees back in the woods. The big lizard had some magic of his own. He called the two boys to him.

"Good morning," said the lizard. "You look tired today."

"We are very tired," said the two boys, "because we cut down ten times ten big trees. But when our father came to see the trees we had cut down, the trees were all growing in the woods again. And now we must cut down ten times ten big trees again."

"I like to hear you sing," said the big lizard. "And if you will sing what I tell you to sing, I will work some magic for you."

And this is what the big lizard told the boys to sing:

"When a boy is a man,

He must do the best he can,

He works and he works,

When the boy is a man."

And as the boys were singing, the lizard danced around them singing:

"Round and round I go.

I draw a magic ring.

I draw a magic red ring.

Round and round I go.

I draw a magic ring.

I draw a magic white ring.

Round and round I go.

I draw a magic ring.

I draw a magic black ring.

Round and round I go.

And now I say, the trees

By the hand of a man

Fall down. Fall down. Fall down.

"You are good boys, and you work like men work. Go and put your hands on the trees, and they will fall down. When your father comes tonight, he will see that you have made a farm for yourself on this side of the woods."

The boys went and put their hands on the trees, and the trees fell down. The boys wanted to sing, and the birds wanted to sing. And the big lizard was very glad.

But the rat and the deer and the rabbit were not glad. They ran and told the old wizard that the trees in the woods were falling down when the boys put their hands on them.

The old wizard was very, very angry. He went to see the owl.

"We must do something right away," said the old wizard. "As soon as the sun is down, the father is coming, and he will see that the boys have cut down ten times ten big trees. Then, he will run me out of the woods."

"I cannot see well in the daytime, so I cannot help you," said the owl. "And, old wizard, you cannot let anyone see your magic in the daytime. So you cannot do anything about the trees when the sun is up. The rat and the deer and the rabbit will have to help you. As fast as the trees fall down, the rat and the deer will have to put them up again."

And the big lizard who saw everything that went on the in the woods saw what the rat and the deer and the rabbit were going to do. The big lizard made some traps. He made a trap for the rat. He made a trap for the deer. He made a trap for the rabbit.

And when the rabbit, with the magic that the wizard had given him, started to put up a tree, the rabbit got his long tail in the trap that the lizard had made. The rabbit jumped and jumped. But he could not get his tail out of the trap. The rabbit jumped and jumped again and again. His tail came off, and he ran away into the woods. The rabbit never had a long tail again, because he helped the old wizard with his magic.

And when the deer, with the magic that the old wizard had given him, began to put up a tree, he got his long tail in the trap that the lizard had made.

The deer jumped and jumped. But he could not get his tail out of the trap. The deer jumped and jumped again and again. His tail came off, and he ran away into the woods. The deer never had a long tail again, because he helped the old wizard with his magic.

And when the rat, with the magic that the old lizard had given him, started to put up a tree, he got his tail in the trap that the lizard had made. Now the rat did not jump and jump. The rat pulled and pulled and pulled. He pulled all the pretty hairs off his tail. And when his tail was out of the trap, the rat ran away to the woods. And from that day to this, the rat has had a long tail with no hairs on it at all.

Then, the old wizard knew that the magic of the lizard was better than his magic. The lizard's magic was kind magic, because he always wanted to help people. The old wizard was so angry that he put on his long, black coat and flew up over the trees and was never seen again.

When the sun was going down, the father came to see what the boys had done. And he saw that the boys had cut down ten times ten big trees, and he was glad.

The boys lived a long, long time on their farm. They liked to sing as they worked. And the birds liked to sing in the trees. And the big lizard was very happy, too.

a
about
afraid
after
again
ahead
alive
all
always
am
an
and
angry
animal
animals
any
anyone
anything
are
around
as
ask
asked
at
away
back
bag
be
bear
bear's
beautiful
because
been
before
began
being
best

better
big
bigger
biggest
bird
birds
black
bottle
boy
boys
brave
bring
brings
buffalo
bugs
but
by
cage
call
called
came
can
cannot
Capa
Capa's
cat
children
clothes
coat
come
comes
coming
could
cover
covered
covering
cow

creatures
cried
cut
cutting
danced
day
days
daytime
deer
did
do
dog
doing
done
door
down
draw
eat
eating
end
every
everything
everywhere
eye
eyes
fall
falling
far
farm
fast
faster
father
fell
fight
fighting
fill
filled

find
first
flew
flowers
fly
foot
for
forget
found
fox
friend
friends
from
funny
gave
gentle
get
give
given
glad
go
goes
going
gone
good
got
grass
great
growing
growl
guanaco
guanacos
had
hairs
hand
hands
happy

hard
has
have
he
head
hear
heard
heels
help
helped
hen
her
here
hill
hills
him
himself
his
hit
hold
hoof
hoofs
horns
horse
house
how
hurt
I
if
in
into
is
it
jump
jumped
just
keep

kept
kill
killed
killing
kind
king
knew
knock
knocked
know
knows
last
laugh
laughed
leg
legs
let
life
like
liked
little
live
lived
lives
living
lizard
lizard's
long
longer
look
looked
looking
looks
lost
love
loved
made

magic

make

man

many

may

me

men

monkey

monkeys

more

morning

mountains

much

must

my

myself

never

night

nip

nipped

nipping

no

nose

not

nothing

now

of

off

oh

old

on

once

one

only

open

opened

or

other

others

our

out

over

owl

own

part

peck

pecked

pecking

people

pick

picked

picking

picks

pig

play

played

playing

please

pretty

pull

pulled

pulling

push

pushed

pushing

put

putting

rabbit

rabbit's

race

ran

rat

red

right

ring
road
round
run
running
said
sat
saw
say
says
scare
see
seen
seven
seventh
shall
she
sheep
shell
should
show
side
sing
singing
sit
sitting
sleep
small
so
some
someone
something
sometimes
sons
soon
South America
split

squirrel
stand
standing
started
stone
stood
stopped
stork
storks
story
street
stronger
strongest
sun
tail
tails
take
taken
talked
teeth
tell
ten
than
thank
that
the
their
them
then
there
these
they
thing
things
think
thinking
this

thought

three

tie

tied

time

times

tired

to

today

toes

together

told

tonight

too

took

top

tops

touch

touched

trap

traps

tree

trees

treetops

try

trying

turn

turned

turtle

turtles

turtle's

two

up

upon

us

used

very

walk

walked

walking

want

wanted

warm

was

watch

watched

water

way

we

well

went

were

what

when

where

whether

white

who

why

will

willing

win

wished

with

without

wizard

wolf

woman

woodpecker

woods

work

worked

working

works

would
yes
you
young
your
yourself